Prayer Treatments
Lightworker's Log

SAM

Third Edition

Copyright © 2014 SAM/Lightworker's Log

All rights reserved.

ISBN 978-1-939890-18-4

Brief quotations embodied in critical articles and reviews allowed. Include the book's title, author's name, and the Lightworker's Log website (LightworkersLog.com) as sources of further information. Contact the author via the above website to comment, for written permission regarding longer excerpts, or to otherwise use or reproduce this book.

Views expressed in this book are solely those of the author. The author makes no warranties as to the accuracy, completeness, timeliness, or usefulness of any information. The author's intent is solely to offer information of a general nature to help you in your quest for emotional and spiritual well-being. The author, publisher, website host, and all parties associated with the book are not responsible for your actions if you choose to use any of the information in this book. In using this book, you agree that any party involved in creating, producing, or delivering it, is not liable for any of the information within. You are solely responsible if you use any of the information in this book for any purpose.

Because of the dynamic nature of the Internet, Web addresses or links contained in this book may have changed since publication and may no longer be valid.

Lovingly dedicated with immense gratitude to the Truth within humanity, One.

Acknowledgements

This book would not exist without the help of family, friends, and spiritual teachers met through classes, workshops, seminars, and conferences. Sincere thanks also go to Cheryl M. Gorder of Eagle Spirit Publishing and Balboa Press for publishing the first editions of *A Change in Perception* and *Lightworker's Log :-) Transformation* from which these Spiritual Mind Treatments originated. I am also thankful for ever-increasing recognition of the Divine Source of *All the Good There Is*, that entity many people call God, which continues to guide those who listen.

Contents

Preface	ix
Author's Note	xii
Successful Use of Prayer Treatments	xiii
Tools to Make a Difference - *Daily Practice*	1
World Healing Meditation (Adapted and Revised)	3
My Gratefulness Log	7
New Lord's Prayer	9
Tools to Make a Difference - *Treatments*	11
Ability to Give and Receive Love	13
Abundance and Prosperity	15
Addiction	17
Arms and Hands	19
Asthma and Hay Fever	21
Bladder	23
Blood Troubles and Skin Dis-eases	25
Clarity of Mind	27
Colds, Flu, and Grippe	29
Constipation	31

Continued Peace, Inner Sight, and Clarity	33
Deafness	35
Diabetes	37
False Growths (Tumors, Cancer, Gallstones)	39
Fatigue Treatment	41
Feet and Legs	43
Fevers	45
Food Security and Safety	47
Headache Treatment	49
Healing Intemperance	51
Health, Peace of Mind, and Unity with Universal Mind	53
Heart Trouble	55
I Put God First Treatment	57
Increased Spiritual Awareness	59
Insanity Treatment	61
Insomnia	63
Irritable Bowel and Bladder	65
Lightworker Treatment for Perfect Health	67
Liver	69

Lung Trouble	71
Nerve Troubles	73
Non-Reaction to Outside Forces	75
Obesity	77
Obstetrics	79
One with Spirit Treatment	81
Pain Treatment	83
Paralysis	85
Peace of Mind	87
Perfect Health	89
Perfect Physical Health	91
Perfect Skin	93
Poison	95
Recovery from Surgery, Diabetes, and High BP	97
Removing the Complex	99
Rheumatism	101
Spiritual Mind Treatment for Children	103
Stability and Conscious Life	105
Stomach and Bowel Troubles	107

Stream of Supply	109
Supply	111
Tranquility and Non-Reaction to Outside Forces	113
Urinary System Perfection	115
Vision Treatment	117
Wake Up to Life Treatment	119
Weather Conditions Treatment	121
Wholeness and Health	123
Epilogue	125
Resources	126
About the Author	127

Preface

First, let me state that I do not work in the health care field nor am I any kind of practitioner. The information in this book comes from my own personal experience. I am merely sharing it with you. Although I have very successfully used many of these structured prayers (also know as Spiritual Mind Treatments), I do not prescribe them for anyone. Nonetheless, since they helped me they may help you.

Energy surrounds us. One of the ways we mold this energy is by thinking. Thoughts hold much more power than ever imagined, constantly playing a major role in what occurs in life. A change in how we look at things makes it possible to change everything, including our state of mind and body. Bodies respond to thoughts so changing the way we think changes the way our body functions.

Maintaining a positive attitude is the first step to health for good thoughts manifest good things. Another way to gain peace of mind, better health, and a more joyful life is to pray. Pray not to something outside that punishes for 'bad' behavior, but to the Vital Life Force within your physicality. Prayers within *Prayer Treatments* suit that intention very well. Repeating prayers helps to make positive changes to our point of view and inner health.

So how did this book come to be? Most people thought I went crazy when my son Daniel passed out of physical form. His transition spurred recognition of the need for change. Life was no longer comfortable and it was time to improve living conditions. Daniel's essence led me through the doors of a Center for Spiritual Living (previously referred to as Science of Mind Center) the year after his transition. Class work assignments and self-study helped to open my mind and consider new thoughts, thereby giving me the key to a new understanding. Increasing awareness of the power of thought helped me to realize that reshaping life was possible. This was welcome information as my dis-eased body dwelled in the land of limitation, pain, and woe. A wide variety of illnesses plagued me, from three "incurable" conditions (interstitial cystitis, osteoarthritis, and spinal deformities – diagnosed though various doctors and repeated medical tests) to lesser inconveniences, such as high blood pressure, irritable bowel syndrome, and gastritis.

Thoughts do indeed shape our world. I learned this first-hand after designing and repeating Spiritual Mind Treatments. They can be very powerful when said by those who embody the principles of our Creator. God (Spirit, Vital Life Force, whatever name you use) is everywhere, and in all of us, ever changing. Treatments help us to recognize and turn to the power of Wholeness within. We then lift thoughts to union with Creation. After all, we are that of which *It* is. We just forgot!

Many of these Spiritual Mind Treatments helped to change thoughts to ones of increasing positivity and spiritual growth. They spurred my transformation from fragmentation to wholeness. I learned how to deal with, and eventually heal dis-ease, with a change in thought patterns. My ever-changing perception blossomed into a pure state of grace, while studying *The Science of Mind* and *A Course In Miracles*. These books make it much easier to progress from a life filled with depression, desperation, illness, and limitation, to one of hope, tranquility, health, and joy.

Spiritual Mind Treatments helped me to reconnect with the unchanging Vital Life Force within, to move beyond ego and fears, and blindly trust that there was more to life than I consciously knew. Increasing awareness of the power within helped to reshape life. Trusting Spirit, I moved beyond ego and fears to finally end decades of prescription drug use. My body began to repair itself with the power of thought and a very, slow, change in lifestyle habits.

After two years of habitually repeating treatments, envisioning an enjoyable unrestricted life, I became completely free of thirteen medications that ruled my small world. And the spinal surgery, suggested by several medical professionals in 2005 to avoid paralysis, is no longer necessary. I am free of many diet restrictions as well.

Now, I truly believe that all things are possible. My quality of life is vastly better and living conditions have immensely improved. I attribute the beginning of this wonderful change to the treatments within this book. After decades of despair, sickness, poverty, and limitation, I now live a hopeful and joyous life of wholeness, excellent health, freedom, and prosperity.

I cannot promise this book will change your life because thoughts, I have learned, are the difference between health and wholeness, love and fear, limitation and prosperity, and various other dualities. However, the good news is that you are in total control of your own thoughts. "What do you have to lose?" Continue your usual medical rituals and use these treatments as something to improve your state of mind. Use the power of thought to shape the body and the world you wish to see. And who knows, you might just find the wholeness and freedom that is already yours!

Author's Note

Thoughts, prayers, and desires feed the Matrix in which we live. There is unseen Power in prayer, regardless of belief. When we pray, prayers merge into a field of unlimited possibility. A Matrix of Good exists even when we don't believe in our own power. I can attest to this fact. This unlimited field of Good surrounds, and connects us, and in doing so, it offers a fertile field to plant thoughts.

Certain capitalized words within *Prayer Treatments* signify aspects or attributes of what many people refer to as *God*. Each treatment ends with "And So *It* Is!" but you can replace this with "Amen" or "So mote it be." Choose the notes and Spiritual Mind Treatments you wish to use. Record the ones that resonate with you, onto a tape recorder, or burn them to a CD or MP3 file. Repeat them in your own voice, feeling the wholeness that you truly are, believing every word. You can then hear them anywhere, at anytime, if you have earphones to fit the recorder or player. Occasionally record them again as your consciousness changes.

You can make a positive difference just by repeating the treatments even if you don't believe every word. When I first started my journey, ego often denied what I repeated. Do not be discouraged if this happens to you. The voice of ego lessens with each repeated treatment, and in time, it's possible to repeat Spiritual Mind Treatments with gusto believing every spoken word. You will find it easier to repeat prayers more enthusiastically after some practice.

I trust *Prayer Treatments* will be of utmost value to you as the process of recognizing Wholeness unfolds. Visit LightworkersLog.com for recorded prayer examples and additional resources.

Successful Use of Prayer Treatments

Spiritual Mind Prayer Treatments are much more successful when you think or say them out loud with great joy. Think of joyful memories. They can be the birth of your children, watching a beautiful sunset with loved ones, enjoying special times with friends, or any number of special moments. Capture that feeling and imprint it within your heart's core. Feel the joy spreading from your heart's core to envelope the entire physical frame. Practice building upon this joyful feeling to bring it forth upon saying the treatment of your choice.

Step One – Repeat a Treatment

When repeating a treatment, remember to radiate your unique, joyful feeling out into your body. Mentally picture yourself at peace, healthy and happy to recognize the perfection within, for within each physical form lies the Wholeness of God, All That Is, whatever term you care to use.

Four Deep Breaths to Seal the Deal

* Next, close your eyes, draw a deep breath of air into your nose, and release it through your mouth, while further expanding the joyful sensation in your heart's core.

* Take another deep breath in through your nose and let that breath out slowly through your mouth.

* Breathe in again and picture a brilliant spark of white Light in the core of your heart. See this spark of wholeness and Truth of your perfection glow and begin to expand as you release the breath through your mouth.

* Take one more deep breath in through your nose, as the brilliant white Light expands throughout your body. Release the breath, though your mouth, and open your eyes.

Now sit quietly, picturing the successful outcome of your treatment. What does it look like? See yourself living life to the fullest degree, on your own terms, expressing the perfection within. If contradictory words fill your mind, thank them for expressing but kindly remind them it's time for a new game, for you are now in charge of your own well-being, able to follow a new, adventurous path of wholeness, peace, joy and abundance in all things good.

Tools to Make a Difference

Daily Practice

World Healing Meditation
(Adapted and Revised)

The *World Healing Meditation* is something I repeated every morning at sunrise, with minor revisions. I note it here because saying it always made me feel good and I'm sure it makes a difference in how we see the world.

Always, always and forever was the Word.
And the Word was *God*.
And God said, "Let there be light" and there was light.

Now is the time of a new beginning.
I AM a Co-Creator with God, and it is Heaven that comes, as the Good Will of God is expressed on Earth through me.
It is the Kingdom of Light, Love, Peace and Understanding.
And I AM doing my part to reveal It's Reality.

I begin with me.
I AM a living Soul and the Spirit of God dwells in me, as me.
I and the Father are One – and all that the Father has is mine.
In Truth, I AM the Christ of God.

What is true of me is true of everyone,
For God is all – and all is God.
I see only the Spirit of God in every Soul.
And to every living thing, I say:
I love you, for you are me. You are my Holy Self.

I now open my heart and let the pure essence of Unconditional Love pour out.
I see it as a Golden Light radiating from the center of my being.
And I feel its Divine Vibration in and through me.
Above, and below me,
Swirling all around me.

I AM One with the Light.
I AM filled with the Light.
I AM illumined by the Light.
I AM the Light of the World.

With purpose of Mind, I send forth the Light.
I let the radiance go before me to join the other Lights.
I know this is happening all over the world.
I see the merging Lights. There is now ONE Light.
We are the LIGHT OF THE WORLD.

The One Light of Love, Peace, and Understanding is moving.
It flows, touching and illuminating every soul in the shadow of the illusion.
And there is only the Light of Reality.

And the radiance grows, permeating, saturating every form of Life.
There is only the vibration of One Perfect Life now.
All living things respond, and the planet is alive with Light and Love.

There is total Oneness. And in the Oneness, we speak the Word.
The sense of separation is now dissolved.
All is returned to Godkind, the real world.

Peace is in every mind.
Love flows forth from every heart.
Forgiveness reigns in every soul.
Understanding is the common bond.

And now, from the Light of the World, the Only Presence and Power responds.
The activity of God is healing and harmonizing all.
Omnipotence is made manifest.

I AM seeing salvation before my very eyes. As all false beliefs and error patterns dissolve. The sense of separation is no more, the Healing has taken place, and all is now restored to sanity.

This is Peace on Earth and Good Will towards all, and love flows forth from every heart – forgiveness reigns in every soul – and all hearts and minds are One in perfect understanding.

It is done.

AND IT IS SO NOW.

Adapted and Revised. Original meditation from: Ft. Lauderdale Church of Religious Science, Science of Mind Center, 1550 NE 26th Street, Ft. Lauderdale, FL 33305, (954) 566-2868, www.RSIFTL.com.

Gratefulness

An attitude of gratefulness always brings greater good. Envision your perfect world even if you do not feel like there is anything to be grateful for now. Put thoughts into words and repeat them at least once a day. As an example, I include my gratefulness log to get you started. After repeating the list every day, I experienced the physical manifestation of everything on this list. And still enjoy the fruits of my labor.

I AM grateful for perfect health, the ability to eat and drink as I please, dance to my hearts delight, and hike through nature joyfully.

I AM grateful for my loving and giving family, all of whom share love and material wealth with one another, are compassionate, and always joyful to spend time with me.

I AM grateful for my friends of like mind who share all things willingly and joyfully (time, material wealth, and knowledge).

I AM grateful for the abundance and prosperity in my life that allows me to have everything I need before I need it, to travel and share my abundance and prosperity with all of humanity, for the greater good of all.

I AM grateful for my generous and considerate husband, who sees the Truth, and values experience enough to do what is right by God's Law.

I AM grateful for the ability to learn and to teach all of humanity in increasingly valuable ways.

I AM grateful to know the Truth. I see Reality and beauty in all things and spread joy, from within me, to everyone I see.

New Lord's Prayer

This is a wonderful prayer, designed by Walter Starke, which I adapted and revised (with one change of the word Higher to Inner). I began to repeat this prayer after taking a class called "It's All God" because it just felt good to break out of the old habit of a Southern Baptist upbringing. The textbook we used was, of course, *It's All God* by Walter Starke.

"My Inner Self, which art Heaven consciousness, wholly be thy recognition. The kingdom of my Inner Self come, Its guidance be done at the outer material level as well as at the inner spiritual level. My Inner Self, fulfill for me all my daily needs, body, mind, and Spirit. Release me when I have not listened to my Inner Self as I release others who are not listening to theirs. Lead me not into the temptation of believing my lower self is all; deliver me from the evil of believing I AM not already One. For this realization of my Inner Self is Heaven, the only power, and the glory of all being.

And So *It* Is!

Source: Walter Starke's *It's All God*, page 173.

Tools to Make a Difference

Treatments

Ability to Give and Receive Love

God is Spontaneous Love, a true love free of all doubt or fear. This Divine Source of Love flows in all living things including myself.

Divine Love fulfills all the Laws of Life. I share this love within my destined relationships from this day forward. There is no doubt that Divine Love flows through me as I express it effectively within my most prominent destined relationships. As this love flows unhindered, unobstructed, and spontaneously within and through me, it is always effectively felt by every person destined to be in my life. Each and every person feeling this Divine Love returns it effectively to its source, twofold. As this Divine Love continues to grow, it clarifies the nature of my True Being and destiny.

I give thanks that the Divine Source of Love consciously works to give me clarity of mind that is free of doubt or fear.

I release this treatment to the Law of Mind, knowing that Divine Love manifests the Thing Itself spontaneously and freely, within and through me.

And So *It* Is!

Abundance and Prosperity

Conscious Life surrounded by Substance flows effortlessly in, and through, me.

The Truth of my Unity with all things successfully draws all that I need to live a self-fulfilled life full of abundance and prosperity. Absolute Law ensures that I AM always richly compensated for all my constructive efforts. Substance always manifests whatever I need before a need arises.

I AM grateful for the ever-flowing abundance and prosperity of whatever it takes to make my life happy and fulfilling. Filled with *All the Good There Is*, and knowing I AM a unique part of the Body of God, I joyously release these words to Universal Mind.

And So *It* Is!

Addiction

The Divine Spirit is within all things. This Self-Knowing Force is complete within the Thing Itself and is never hindered. It is the voice of reason, harmony, and clarity, full of *All the Good There Is*.

This Divine Spirit lives within me, and using its Infinite Intelligence, manifests *All the Good There Is*. I AM full of positivity, good health, compassion, and a feeling of harmonious unity with all living things.

I declare that Absolute Intelligence manifests peace and limitless opportunity for growth through me, resulting in Perfection without any desire for unnatural substances, alcohol, illegal drugs, or fear of any kind.

I AM grateful to the Divine Source of All Good for the gifts that I manifest, with the power of Divine Universal Intelligence.

With joyful and complete trust in God, our Creator, I entrust these words to the Law of Mind knowing that I AM free, for I know the truth of my real being.

And So *It* Is!

Arms and Hands

God is in all things. This Divine BEing flows freely throughout my physical body and spirit.

I AM filled with creative ideas as this Life Essence offers me the ability to reach out and grasp Reality. My faith and conviction of Truth is firmly rooted within and I partake of the Divine Benefits that God offers to all living things.

The power of Infinite Intelligence flows freely as I gratefully acknowledge God steadily in my life.

With knowledge of Absolute Intelligence and Conscious Volition, I release this treatment to the Law of God.

And So *It* Is!

Asthma and Hay Fever

The One and Only Infinite Mind is my mind, inspired with perfection and *All the Good There Is*. I AM open and sensitive to the flow of good in my higher consciousness.

My conscious mind expresses my divine inheritance. It is filled with thoughts of love, joy, and peace. My body is the Temple of the Holy Ghost and I recognize my Oneness with Infinite Life. Nothing obstructs the perfect functioning of my entire body. The Law of Spirit flows freely, exhilarating and vitalizing me. There is only perfect calm as my thoughts are clarified in the Universal Mind.

I AM thankful to know that the breath of God is my breath flowing unrestricted through channels of pure receptivity from Infinite Intelligence.

I release this treatment to the Law of God as I breathe in the Eternal Life Essence that purifies me and keeps me strong.

And So *It* Is!

Bladder

Eternal Life is mine as I recognize the Conscious Life flowing in and through me.

The Principle of Life acts through me filling my body with positivity, peace, and perfection in all its forms. My thoughts remain calm and free of worry, as the purity and strength of Infinite Reality stops stress, and insecurity, from entering my mind. Perfect assimilation, and appropriate elimination of body substances, occurs as Divine Order guides all body functions.

With joyous peace of mind, I thankfully acknowledge the Infinite Mind that ensures wholeness. Recognizing that I AM an expression of God-Mind, an example of the dynamic Principle of Life, I consciously release these words to flow freely throughout Universal Mind.

And So *It* Is!

Blood Troubles and Skin Dis-eases

The One and Only Infinite Reality lives in all things and flows freely within me.

The rhythmic harmony of my life acknowledges that I AM a temple of God-Life. As Divine Light and Energy freely flow, I AM ageless and deathless, always abiding in God's Law. My blood manifests as pure and perfect Spiritual Substance. The Divine Source of Spirit flows perfectly through my bloodstream keeping it pure. Consciousness of Life fills me with Divine Love and Harmony for all living things.

I AM one in essence and experience with *All the Good There Is*. My bloodstream constantly renews as Spiritual Substance continues to manifest love, peace, and harmony fulfilling my every need. A calm Self-Propelling Life-Force perfectly revitalizes my entire body with pure Spiritual Substance.

I thank the One and Only Infinite Reality knowing the nature of my real being. Joyous self-realization of Spirit fills me with gratefulness for my Spiritual Perfection.

I release this treatment to Spirit knowing that Absolute Intelligence and Divine Law spread these words throughout the Universe.

And So *It* Is!

Clarity of Mind

God is everywhere including the Creative Energy that surrounds us. As a unique part of this God-Life, I AM a perfect point of God-Conscious Life. The essence of all healing power flows through me, as I am a vessel of God.

Clarity of Mind is apparent in all that I experience.

Gratefulness overwhelms my essence as I release these words to the Creative Energy to work through Absolute Law.

And so It is.

Colds, Flu, and Grippe

The Life of God flows freely, in and through, all things. This Life Force manifests *All the Good There Is* through me.

Every breath I take verifies my unity with Infinite Life. Conscious Life affords me clarity of thought. My mind is full of harmony, confidence, and understanding. God sustains me in perfect health at all times, bringing me peace of mind, and freeing me from harm. Unification and spiritual perfection fulfill my every need.

I AM grateful for my peace of mind and a free heart filled with the Law of Spirit. Recognizing Absolute Law guides my life, I release these words freely into the Creative Energy of Universal Mind.

And So *It* Is!

Constipation

The Origin of *All the Good There Is* flows freely with Absolute Intelligence offering unconditional Love, Truth, and Wholeness to all people. I feel this Divine BEing within me as the free flow of Life Essence constantly guides every aspect of my life.

All my life forces are harmonious, normal, and perfect as my body functions while Infinite Intelligence rules. There is no fear, no congestion, restriction, inaction, or dis-ease as my body functions perfectly. I recognize the true nature of my being and accept it without resistance. My actions are firmly rooted in Reality, Divine Love, and Truth. My muscles, and bowel, functions with ease acknowledging the Principle of Unity.

God's presence insures the free flow of Life Essence and I AM eternally thankful. Knowing this treatment works by Absolute Law, I release it to Universal Intelligence.

And So *It* Is!

Continued Peace, Inner Sight, and Clarity

The Supreme Personality of the Universe is in all things. As a unique part of this Divine BEing, I AM free of all limitation.

Absolute Intelligence ensures a Divinely Sustained Stream of fearless Peace that consciously relaxes my essence at all times. Clarity of Mind continues to increase God-Life and my spiritual vision glows as the rays of the Sun. My spirit's destiny is fulfilled on this earth, through Divine Timing. Continued faith in the Divine Mind ensures the fulfillment of my spirit's destiny in the afterlife, with conscious ease, and abandonment of all earthly outcomes.

"Father, I commend my spirit to thee."

Thankful for ever-increasing recognition of the Law of Unity, I never waver or sway from the nature of my True Being and destiny. The Divine Source of *All the Good There Is* constantly fills my spirit with gratefulness, joy, and freedom from earthly outcomes. I gratefully retain conscious knowledge of my True Being and all lessons, and experiences, obtained from the beginning of time, forevermore.

Recognizing the Power of Absolute Law, my spirit humbly accepts Infinite Life, and sees the Law of God as the Creative Energy that accepts these words to eternally flow throughout all space.

And So *It* Is!

Deafness

The truth of my real being is now revealed as Divine Harmony fills me with *All the Good There Is*.

This Divine Harmony fills my physical being with an ever-increasing capacity to make positive life choices. I AM filled with confidence, and always receptive to changes, ever conscious of Absolute Intelligence. Divine Mind affords me the luxury of perfect, complete, Divine ideas, which I faithfully accept to increase my spiritual growth. I co-operate, knowing the Truth that promotes perfect hearing, for God hears through me. Every idea I have functions according to Divine Law.

I AM thankful, open, and receptive to the Divine Harmony that allows me to hear the voice of God. I release this treatment, as both ears remain open and receptive to the vibration of Perfect Harmony.

And So *It* Is!

Diabetes

Spirit is the origin of *All*. I feel and recognize the God-Life that fills my consciousness.

The Truth keeps my body free of dis-ease. All the food I eat is perfectly suited to meet my body needs. The food is absorbed and digested normally, filling every atom of my body with joy, and fulfillment. My blood stream carries the foods energy, and gives me all I need for perfect body function, as it ensures that my blood is pure.

Perfect conscious awareness of the Divine Mind is gratefully acknowledged as I release this treatment to Universal Intelligence.

And So *It* Is!

False Growths (Tumors, Cancer, Gallstones)

I recognize my True Being as part of One Creative Mind forever manifesting Divine Love and perfection.

This Eternal Presence consciously cleanses my blood, keeping my body in harmony with positivity, and creative ideas full of *All the Good There Is*. Receptive Intelligence guides the free flow of Life Essence, which assures that every atom in my body is perfect. Absolute Intelligence maintains the perfection within with sustained faith and trust in God, our Creator.

I AM thankful that Spirit is completely manifested as perfection within my True Being.

With recognition of the Eternal Presence in me, I release this treatment to the Law of God.

And So *It* Is!

Fatigue Treatment

God is Infinite Strength, full of energy, and peace. This Changeless Reality is in all things including me.

Infinite Strength flows freely throughout my body uprooting anything incompatible with peace. This Infinite Strength is in my consciousness at all times, keeping me vital and strong. The Self-Knowing Mind affords me with clarity of thought at all times.

Infinite Strength resides within me forevermore and I AM eternally grateful. I release this treatment to Universal Intelligence as the Principle of Unity freely guides my life.

And So *It* Is!

Feet and Legs

The ever-present Mind works by Absolute Law. It is in all things. The Infinite Reality of this power flows freely within me.

I AM guided by the ever-present Mind towards *All the Good There Is*. My ability to walk and continuously evolve is guided by right action and truth in all that I do.

The Power of Spirit fills me with humility and gratefulness as I recognize Its glory. By releasing this treatment to Universal Intelligence, I shall always be guided into all truth led by the ever-present Mind.

And So *It* Is!

Fevers

The Indwelling Almighty flows unhindered in me.

I AM conscious of my oneness with God who constantly fills me with peace and comfort of mind. The Law of Spirit allows access to only positive thoughts. Conscious Life boosts my faith as I continue to experience *All the Good There Is*.

I AM thankful for my Divinity, which is a safe haven that allows me to consciously be one with the Indwelling Almighty.

Fearlessly, I release this treatment to the Law of Spirit allowing these words to flow in the wind and fill all space.

And So *It* Is!

Food Security and Safety

Law of Spirit guides every aspect of my life, even the choices I make to fill my human host.

The Truth ensures that I always have the nourishment needed to keep my body strong. Every dietary choice I make is based on the way Spirit works through Creative Energy. I always consume healthy and appropriate food and drink, omitting substances that may be harmful to my physical body, or the spirit within.

I consume nourishing food and fluids knowing they are my Spiritual Substance and supply. All of these spiritual substances are one with the Essence of Conscious Life, filled with Absolute Intelligence. All nourishment is healing, and works in harmony with Spirit, to fill and always renew me with *All the Good There Is*.

I gratefully recognize the Absolute Law that guides my food and drink choices. I release these words to the Law of God to freely flow within, and through, Universal Intelligence.

And So *It* Is!

Headache Treatment

The Consciousness of God flows through all people. This Infinite Intelligence is within me filling my brain cells with peace.

The vitalizing power of the Divine Spirit fills me with clarity of mind, allowing my entire body to relax, free from worry or confusion. Infinite Intelligence guides my emotions to right thinking.

I AM grateful for the Consciousness of God within me at all times.

The flow of Life Force is unretarded, and sustained throughout eternity, as I release this treatment to the Law of Mind with complete ease.

And So *It* Is!

Healing Intemperance

The Beloved is in all things and fills me with Divine Love and Tranquility. I AM positive, acting freely at all times, as my unity with God is everlasting.

I act appropriately and fearlessly, free of any limitation, during all situations. Conscious Life fills me with faith and joy meeting all needs. Recognition of Divine Reality fills me with *All the Good There Is*. I AM always satisfied with how God guides every aspect of my life.

I AM grateful for the Truth of Infinite Reality that constantly supplies me with Creative Energy. Releasing these words to the Law of God, completeness and satisfaction are mine forevermore. I bask in the light of Infinite Life.

And So *It* Is!

Health, Peace of Mind, and Unity with Universal Mind

God is perfect health, perfect peace, and limitless love. This Divine Source flows through all things including me.

The presence of Infinite Intelligence operates freely within me stopping all negativity. Perfection flows through my blood, as I AM one with Divine Mind. Spirit allows me to grow. All negative senses are effortlessly replaced with a warm sense of my Oneness in essence, and experience, with *All the Good There Is*.

I give thanks to God that I AM guided by Infinite Intelligence clearing all thought of limitation.

Perfection manifests the Thing Itself within me throughout eternity as I release this treatment to the Law of Mind.

And So *It* Is!

Heart Trouble

The Body of God is perfect. It is Divine Love, which flows unhindered throughout all things.

Divine Law and Harmony continually guide my life. Infinite Intelligence supports all body functions, and my heart is a living center, through which Divine Love eternally flows. My heart is never troubled for the blood in my veins and arteries flow freely. This heart healthy action results in perfect circulation, assimilation, and elimination of the lifeblood in me. Universal Mind counteracts negative thoughts as I recognize I AM ageless Spirit.

Recognizing this Law of Life within me, I AM grateful for the way that Spirit works.

I AM one with Conscious Life, and release this treatment to the Universal Mind knowing that I AM because, It is.

And So *It* Is!

I Put God First Treatment

God is all there is. As a part of this Divine BEing, all life is perfect, whole, and complete.

Every action I perform is for the highest good of All. I consciously choose to put God first in all ways, as I, along with all life, am a part of God.

I AM grateful for this Truth and for the clarity of Mind that allows this Truth to be known.

Releasing this treatment to the Creative Energy that flows through all space, I AM assured that it is so.

And So *It* Is!

Increased Spiritual Awareness

The Living Spirit Almighty is within all things guiding every action towards *All the Good There Is*. This Divine BEing is firmly rooted in me, a point of God-conscious life, Truth, and Divine Harmony.

I AM a center in the Divine Mind and faith neutralizes all fear, doubt, or negativity within me. Everything I do, say, or think is stimulated by the Truth of my real being. Effortless actions animate everything I do, say, or think toward *All the Good There Is*. I AM guided by Absolute Law and my affairs are guarded in right action. Divine Harmony with all things enhances feelings of positivity, happiness, perfect health, and complete satisfaction.

I AM filled with *All the Good There Is* and always guided by Absolute Intelligence. I AM thankful for the way Spirit works in my life forever fulfilling me with a sense of peace and Divine Unity with *All the Good There Is*. Divine Reality of the Principle of Unity is recognized, and received, with conscious gratefulness.

As I release these words to the Law of God, I AM assured that I AM forevermore guided by Absolute Intelligence.

And So *It* Is!

Insanity Treatment

The Mind of God is the only Mind there is. This Mind is Perfect, Whole, and Complete. This Mind is in all people including myself.

I AM conscious of the Perfect Presence of the Mind of God that circulates through me. My thoughts are always rational and poised. This Divine Sense of the Universal Mind affords me with clarity of thought, which flows in unlimited supply in all of my brain cells.

With peaceful clarity of Mind, I give thanks to the Origin of All for my consciousness that is in perfect concert with the Mind of God.

I AM eternally thankful for the Principle of Unity that recognizes the Mind of God as my own and release this treatment to *It*.

And So *It* Is!

Insomnia

As the earth moves to reveal the rays of the Sun, and the light filled stillness of the Moon, I know God is a part of me.

The Sun's rays melt the snow, and heat renews the plants below ground, while perfect trust in God relaxes and renews my body. I let go of earthly thoughts and rest in the Body of God. My entire body overflows with peace and Divine Tranquility. It ceaselessly ensures the stillness in me with ease. Divine Wisdom fills me as I rest in the still silence of Spirit. I remain divinely protected.

My body is richly blessed with Divine Love, full of goodness. I happily rejoice, and thank the Origin of All, as nothing disturbs my spiritual self. Spirit always takes care of my affairs.

The all-powerful Mind of the Indwelling Christ within fills me with Eternal Peace, as I consciously release these words, to soar through the winds of Universal Intelligence.

And So *It* Is!

Irritable Bowel and Bladder

The Supreme Personality of the Universe includes all life. I AM a part of this Divine Spirit.

As the Divine Mind guides me towards *All the Good There Is*, my thoughts remain calm. My gastrointestinal tract and urinary system reflect the wholeness of God. They perform perfectly, constantly adjusting to their natural and spiritual perfection and operation. My bowels, bladder, kidneys, and their organs are perfect, for they are spiritual ideas and all that God conceived is perfect. Perfect elimination occurs, as my thoughts remain calm. No waste substance remains and my body is cleansed, of all impurities, regularly and normally.

I AM grateful for the power of Absolute Law that fills me with Divine Love, peace and harmony for all things.

Recognizing the Unity of Good, I release this treatment to the Law of God knowing that my gastrointestinal tract and urinary system both operate in their perfect and natural state.

And So *It* Is!

Lightworker Treatment for Perfect Health

I recognize the nature of our Creator as being One Infinite Intelligence operating in effortless Perfection, ever expanding, growing, and nurturing the manifestations of the Divine Mind.

I AM a manifestation of the Mind of God operating in healthy and effortless perfection. Infinite Intelligence, free of any limitation, guides me. It is my nature to expand and grow easily accepting, that, which nurtures my evolution. My life is a quest to nurture human evolution and serve our Creator with Love, Peace, and Harmony among all things. I welcome the knowledge I receive in achieving this honor.

I am grateful to Spirit as I recognize there is no limitation of any sort. I thank the Divine Source of *All the Good There Is* for the gifts I receive daily.

With effortless acceptance, I entrust these words to the Laws of the Universe, the Law of Mind, to flow eternally throughout all space.

And So *It* Is!

Liver

I AM conscious of the One Divine Power and Vital Essence within.

Divine Harmony, guided by Absolute Law, fills every cell of my body with perfection. Divine Mind clarifies thoughts of harmony and unity with all things. The Beloved molds all new matter that flows into my physical form as pleasant memory experiences. These experiences continually renew themselves with ease. The Law maintains an orderly balance of harmonious thoughts that form ideas, which heal, cleanse, and uplift my Spirit.

Easily releasing this treatment to the Law of God, I AM grateful to recognize the One Divine Power and Vital Essence within me.

And So *It* Is!

Lung Trouble

The Life of God is the One Infinite Life and Substance. It is my life now, flowing in and through me, eternally.

My breath is the Life and Light of God, perfectly flowing through my bronchial tubes, my trachea, and my lungs. As my breath flows, it is perfectly expressed as Absolute Intelligence. Each breath expresses my faith and trust in *All the Good There Is*, which constantly renews the flow of the One Infinite Life and Substance in me.

I AM grateful for the Principle of Unity that continues to demonstrate my oneness with God. Peacefully, and in Perfect Confidence, I entrust this treatment to the Law of God knowing that the all-powerful Essence of Spirit maintains my breath, and entire body.

And So *It* Is!

Nerve Troubles

God, the Living Spirit, is the only Presence in all things. I AM a part of this pure, perfect, and harmonious Spirit. I recognize my nerves are the highest form of intelligence.

I abide in faith as Spirit runs through my flesh. The Essence of Life flows freely and peacefully within, as thoughts of poise and power occur, without strain or struggle. The all-powerful Mind of the Indwelling Christ fills me with love, protection, fearless power, peace, strength, and *All the Good There Is*. The One Mind in me continues to renew my faith and keep my nerves firm, steady and sensitive, quickly responding appropriately at all times. The steady presence of the One Power dwells in me. I AM complete and confident as my awareness of the one final Reality continues to increase.

My body functions according to Divine Law and I live in a sea of Perfect Life poised in eternal calm. Spirit manifests in me as perfect harmony because the Law of God governs every atom in my body.

I AM thankful to recognize that the past, present, and future are an unbroken stream of Good, and God is the light, power, and inspiration of my life. My past and future are continuations of the one unbroken chain of life, yet no past brings discord to the present.

I release this treatment to the Universal Consciousness as my cup of acceptance fills, and overflows, with the manifestations of my desires.

And So *It* Is!

Non-Reaction to Outside Forces

The Supreme Personality of the Universe includes all things. My perfection within the Divine Spirit is pure Unity.

Divine Mind guides me towards *All the Good There Is*. All thoughts remain calm. My non-reaction reflects unity with Divine Tranquility. Divine Love, peace, and harmony constantly flow freely as Absolute Law assures ever-present Infinite Tranquility. Spirit fuels positive thoughts and as a part of Spirit, I AM always free of irritation or agitation. Positive interactions with all people constantly occur. Divine Harmony reflects my attitude as the rays of the Sun at all times.

Recognizing that the Divine Mind is my mind, Spirits gifts of Love, Peace, Harmony and Perfection constantly spur thoughts of thanks.

These words now flow through the Law of God and the Law of Unity eternally throughout all space.

And So *It* Is!

Obesity

First Cause, the Body of God, is my body, now manifesting symmetry and perfection.

I AM complete. My body is a part of Spirit, always dependable, using Absolute Law to meet my needs. Divine order guides my appetite. The foods I eat are perfectly absorbed and digested. Gods Divine Love, care, and substance fill the food I eat, in perfect proportion. Spirit fulfills my every need, fearlessly expressing the Thing Itself, with full recognition of Divine Love.

I AM thankful for the presence of God in my life. I release this treatment to Universal Intelligence with presence of mind, aware that Spirit works in, and through, me.

And So *It* Is!

Obstetrics

I rest in Infinite Reality, unified with Absolute Intelligence, and give myself peacefully to the care of Perfection in action.

Right action prevails as the Creative Law working in me synchronizes the growth and perfection of the baby I carry in my womb. Absolute Law allows Absolute Intelligence to ensure that every atom in this new body is healthy, on every plane of expression. Creative Energy works perfectly, as I remain serene and calm, free of negative thought.

I AM grateful to know that the great Law of Creation always operates at the correct time. I joyfully release this treatment to the Law of Spirit.

And So *It* Is!

One with Spirit Treatment

The One and Only Infinite Mind is my mind. It is perfect and filled with Light, *All the Good There Is*.

I AM open to the flow of good in my higher mind. My conscious mind is filled with thoughts of love, joy, peace and *All the Good There Is*. I AM always perfectly calm and filled with the Truth of the Universe. My belief in Universal Mind guides everything I do, say, or think.

Life is always good for me. I AM always healthy and happy, having whatever I need, because I AM filled with love for everything. I have many friends and we help each other passionately enjoy life and be positive. Divine Mind guides all my actions to do what is right. Truth floods me with peace and oneness for I AM always guided by the One Mind of all people.

Knowing my words are now part of the Universe, I thank the one and Only Infinite Mind.

And So *It* Is!

Pain Treatment

God is present in all things. This Creative Energy flows easily within and through me. As this Perfect Presence circulates in every cell of my body, it spreads a Divine sense of peace and ease.

I AM grateful for the freely flowing stream of fearless peace that operates through the power of Absolute Law.

I release this treatment to Creative Mind, the Law of God, knowing that Divine Peace is within me forevermore.

And So *It* Is!

Paralysis

Conscious Life is in all things. This Infinite Reality is within me using the Dependable and Action Principle, which affords me perfect freedom to vitalize my perfect body. Clarity of mind reveals my oneness with the Divine Mind. My endeavors are always guided in right action.

There are no thoughts of restriction or limitation as my mind remains peaceful, calm, and devoid of any turmoil. Infinite Life and Action reveals the true nature of my being.

I AM thankful for the presence of life, and right action in my life, as the Universal Force flows freely within me.

Aware of the One Indwelling Presence, the free-flowing life of Spirit, I AM eternally free releasing this treatment to Universal Mind.

And So *It* Is!

Peace of Mind

God is Divine Tranquility. I AM pleased to be a part of the Origin of All for Infinite Intelligence is the only cause, medium, and effect in my life.

The Principle of Peace flows freely within assuring a sense of confidence and tranquility. My mind is full of Truth and assurance of completeness and perfection. I trust the Law of Spirit to bring good into my life, as Peace and Light guide me towards *All the Good There Is*.

Aware of my unity with Universal Intelligence, I AM grateful to be Christ, the Son within the Body of God.

Rejoicing in my perfection, knowing that Divine Tranquility and Love guide every aspect of my life, I release this treatment to the Law of Spirit.

And So *It* Is!

Perfect Health

God is perfect health, perfect peace, and limitless love, free of all dis-ease, discord, or disharmony. This Divine Source flows through all things including me. Right where pain, dis-ease, discord, resentment, anger, or fear seems to operate, the presence of Infinite Intelligence is.

Perfection flows through my blood, as I AM one with Divine Mind. Spirit allows me to grow. There is no inner agitation or outward irritation in me. A warm sense of my Oneness, in essence and experience with *All the Good There Is*, replaces inner agitation or outward irritation.

I give thanks to God that I AM guided by Infinite Intelligence clearing all thought of limitation. I release this treatment to the Law of Mind knowing that Perfection manifests Itself, within me, forevermore throughout eternity.

And So *It* Is!

Perfect Physical Health

I recognize the Living Spirit Almighty as perfect, indestructible, and indispensable. This Perfect Presence circulates in every cell of my body.

My consciousness of God fills me with Divine Love, peace, harmony, and *All the Good There Is*. Infinite Intelligence guides every aspect of my life and sustains my true Perfect BEing at all times. I AM full of creative ideas, positivity, clarity of mind, and inner sight. This affords me the gift of unhindered faith in the Spiritual Substance that sustains my body's perfection.

I AM grateful for the constant flow of the perfect One Infinite Life and Substance within me. Aware of the Principle of Unity that consistently demonstrates my oneness with *All the Good There Is*, I entrust this treatment to the Law of God.

And So *It* Is!

Perfect Skin

The one and only Self-Knowing Spirit is within all people. This Life Essence is within me.

A great sense of calmness freely flows through me since I recognize the Truth of my True Being as peace and harmony. The Consciousness of God constantly renews my entire being, relaxing me with thoughts of *All the Good There Is*.

I AM thankful that the one and only Self-Knowing Spirit is an active part of my True Being. With calmness, peace, and harmony for all things, I release this treatment to the Law of God knowing that Absolute Intelligence guides every aspect of my life.

And So *It* Is!

Poison

My body is pure Spirit Substance for the One and Only Substance flows within.

This Perfect and Pure Life of God circulates freely to assure that body organs manifest my oneness with Spirit. The blood of my body is forever pure, perfect, and circulating freely. I AM full of positivity and *All the Good There Is*.

The pure Life of God flows in and through me always creating a sense of gratitude and I thank *All the Good There Is*.

Infinite Reality allows me to see my Unity with the Spirit of Life as I release this treatment to the Universal Mind.

And So *It* Is!

Recovery from Surgery, Diabetes, and High Blood Pressure

I AM one with the Living Spirit Almighty. Dis-ease has no avenue to express itself for Spirit is always actively operating through me.

My body is operating perfectly in tune with *All the Good There Is* and I AM guided effortlessly into all Truth. I AM filled with peace, poise, and power, always harmonious with the One Power of Spirit. Every atom of my body is complete and perfect, now and forevermore, filled with the essence of Pure Thought.

A consciousness of perfect love, harmony, and peace constantly renews the stream of life within me. My body overflows with a warm sense of Oneness, in essence and experience, with *All the Good There Is*. Spirit circulates freely within me.

Releasing these words to Universal Intelligence, I AM grateful to be led by the ever-present Mind.

And So *It* Is!

Removing the Complex

The One and Only Divine BEing lives in all things. I AM a part of this Perfect Essence.

My consciousness is based on Divine Truth, which fills me with *All the Good There Is*, and gives me clarity of thought. There is no room in my mind for opposing thoughts because my inner consciousness reigns supreme. All of my actions are based on the Truth of Divine Mind as Creative Energy continually guides each and every thought. The Law of Mind ensures that my thoughts are harmonious, peaceful, and trusting.

I AM grateful for the Absolute Intelligence that feeds my belief in the Universal Mind, which manifests through me.

As Divine Truth fills my mind with a constant flow of Creative Energy, I release this treatment to the Law of God.

And So *It* Is!

Rheumatism

I AM a spiritual being within the Body of God, perfect and free. Divine Tranquility assures the Infinite Reality that I AM.

Eternal Truth and beauty are mine as I sense the sunshine in my soul. Divine Intelligence guides me. Divine Law eliminates impurities. My body is full of Truth and freely allows the power of Creative Energy to circulate in my conscious mind. Body fluids flow effortlessly as I AM aware of Divine Love for all things.

I thank the Living Spirit Almighty for the Divine Love that flows, in and through me, as perfect rays of sunshine. Gratefully, with perfect clarity of mind, I release these words to soar though the wind filling all space.

And So *It* Is!

Spiritual Mind Treatment for Children

The One and Only Knowing Living Spirit surrounds, and lives, in all. This Perfect BEing manifests Itself without limitation through all children living on earth.

Harmony and spontaneous Unity, Positivity, Divine compassion, Complete satisfaction, and Perfect Health flow through all earth children as they are one with God.

The Living Spirit Almighty freely guides every aspect of life for all earth children towards *All the Good There Is*. Fearless faith in the Creative Mind frees all thought of limitation.

I AM grateful to the Divine Source of all good for the gifts of Harmony, Unity, Positivity, Compassion, Complete satisfaction, and Perfect Health that manifest within all earth children.

I release this treatment and entrust it to the Law of Mind secure in the Truth of One Mind manifesting the Spirit of the Universe within all things forever.

And So *It* Is!

Stability and Conscious Life

(Author's Note: If you wish, you can replace the word children with the name of a specific child. I have used the name Mary to show you how to do this.)

The Living Spirit Almighty is within all things guiding every action towards *All the Good There Is*. This Divine BEing is firmly rooted in children (Mary), points (a point) of God-conscious life, Truth, and Divine Harmony.

Children (Mary) are (is) a center in the Divine Mind and faith neutralizes all fear, doubt, or negativity within them (her). Everything children (Mary) do (does), say (says) or think (thinks) is stimulated by the Truth of their (her) real Being. Effortless actions animate everything they (she) do (does), say (says), or think (thinks) towards *All the Good There Is*.

Children (Mary) are (is) well liked by their (her) peers, who enjoy their (her) companionship, and interact with them (her) in mutually positive and nurturing ways. Absolute Law guides children (Mary) and their (her) affairs are guarded in right action. Divine Harmony with all things enhances children's (Mary's) feelings of self-worth, positivity, happiness, perfect health, and complete satisfaction. Children (Mary) are (is) filled with *All the Good There Is* and always guided by Absolute Intelligence.

I AM thankful for the way Spirit works in the children's (Mary's) life, forever filling them (her) with a sense of peace, and Divine Unity with *All the Good There Is*. Divine Reality of the Principle of Unity is recognized and received with conscious gratefulness.

As I release these words to the Law of God, I AM assured that Absolute Intelligence forevermore guides children (Mary).

And So *It* Is!

Stomach and Bowel Troubles

I recognize the Beloved in every atom of my being. My faith, perfect and complete, fills me and elates my entire body.

I AM filled with *All the Good There Is*. Divine Love guides my thinking. Divine Mind elevates my thoughts relaxing them along with my entire body, including all the muscles in my gastrointestinal tract. I give freely of myself and time, unselfishly. I AM filled with love, joy, and positivity. I eat my food thankfully and calmly, free of any discord. The food I eat is absorbed, digested, and assimilated perfectly.

I AM grateful knowing that the very life of God vitalizes my entire body. The Principle of Life fills me with Infinite Life and Eternal Perfection.

I release this treatment to the Law of God, as Life Spirit flows through me, working by Absolute Law to renew me continually.

And So *It* Is!

Stream of Supply

I am surrounded by pure Spirit, God, the Living Spirit Almighty. My thought is God thought, the Law of God for I AM of *It*. I have an inner understanding of my place in the Universe. The Divine has not incarnated in anyone else in just the same way that *It* has in me. I AM, and remain, forever my true Self, united with all Selves, but always unique and individualized.

The Living Spirit of Love and right action leads, guides, and inspires me. All good is now manifest in my experience. I have an abundance of whatever it takes to make life happy and opulent. Everything I do is a success and I am compensated well for all my efforts. I am compelled to move in the right direction and always know where to go, what to do, and how to do it. Substance surrounds me, always taking the form of supply, and manifesting itself to me in the form of whatever my need may be at the time.

A continuous movement of all that I need to express the fullest life, happiness, and action always flows toward me. There is that in me, which all people recognize as worthwhile and desirable. Everyone I meet loves this unique self of mine and recognizes its worth. I draw all toward me and those whom I can benefit, and those who can benefit me, irresistibly draw toward me. I know. The Truth makes me totally free and my life is unlimited in all that is good.

I see that everything, which is desirable, must be a spiritual idea, and I always have this idea right in my mind. This idea of abundance is mine and I take it now, and forevermore. I am at all times compelled to know, accept, and operate upon ever-present opportunity for self-expression and compensation. I have abundance because I am abundance. All that the Father hath is mine.

I am truly grateful for these truths as I release these words to the Law of God knowing it is so.

And so *It* is!

This treatment is adapted from page 263 of *The Science of Mind* by Ernest Holmes.

Supply

Conscious Life, surrounded by Substance, flows effortlessly to supply all my needs. The Truth of my unity with all things successfully draws people like me, to me, and we enrich each other's life.

The Living Spirit of Divine Love guides every aspect of my life, at all times, in the right direction. My constructive endeavors reflect unity with all things. Divine Love ensures that I AM compensated for all my efforts. Spiritual Substance always manifests whatever I need before a need arises. I always have an abundance of whatever it takes to make my life happy and fulfilling.

I AM thankful for the conscious understanding of Divine BEing, which fulfills all needs at all times. Filled with *All the Good There Is*, and knowing that I AM a unique part of the Body of God, I joyously release these words to the Universal Mind.

And So *It* Is!

Tranquility and Non-Reaction to Outside Forces

The Supreme Personality of the Universe includes all life. I AM a segment of this Divine Spirit.

My thoughts remain calm as Divine Mind guides me towards *All the Good There Is*. I do not react to outside forces for Spirit freely guides every aspect of my life. Divine Love, Peace, and Harmony grow within as I have positive interactions with all living things. There is no worry, anxiety, or fear of criticism because my mind is part of the Divine Mind that fuels all thoughts and actions. My body is free of all negativity, pain, irritation, or agitation.

I AM grateful for the Power of Absolute Law that fills me with Divine Love, Peace and Harmony for all things.

Recognizing the Unity of Good, I release this treatment to the Law of God to flow eternally throughout all space.

And So *It* Is!

Urinary System Perfection

The Supreme Personality of the Universe includes all life. I AM a part of this Divine Spirit.

My bladder, kidneys and their organs are perfect because they are spiritual ideas and all that God conceived is perfect. Thoughts remain calm as Divine Mind guides me towards *All the Good There Is*. Security, ease, and reassurance replace all thoughts of dis-ease. My entire urinary tract performs perfectly. It constantly adjusts to its natural and spiritual perfection and operation. Perfect elimination occurs, as my thoughts remain calm. My body is cleansed of all impurities normally.

I AM grateful for the power of Absolute Law that fills me with Divine Love, peace, and harmony for all things.

Recognizing the Unity of Good, I release this treatment to the Law of God, knowing that my urinary system operates in its perfect and natural state.

And So *It* Is!

Vision Treatment

Our Creator sees all things with perfect clarity through its Divine Mind. This Divine Mind is in me filling me with *All the Good There Is.*

My soul is filled with pure light as clarity of mind realizes my oneness with God. Inner sight affords me the gift of spiritual vision and unhindered faith in spiritual substance. My perfect eyes reflect the clearness of spiritual vision and I see perfection in all creation.

I AM grateful that my eyes animate with the light of love, joy, faith, and noble service to humanity.

As I lift up my eyes unto God, from whom comes my perfect sight, I release this treatment to Creative Mind, the Law of Spirit.

And So *It* Is!

Wake Up to Life Treatment - W(orld) A(ll good) K(arma) E(ternity) – U(nity) P(eace) to L(ove) I(nfinity) F(orgiveness) E(volution)

The Supreme Personality of the Universe is in all things. This Spirit (Adhi, Adon, Adonai, Agni, Allah, Atman, Beloved, Brahman, Divine BEing, Divine Love, Divine Spirit, First Cause, God, Great I AM, Illah, Indra, Ishwara, It, Jehovah, Kami, Lord, Mind, Nature, One & Only, Reality, Rita, Saguna, Spirit, Supreme Personality of the Universe, Theo, Uaruna, Yahweh, and so on…) is everywhere. I AM a part of this Divine Spirit that is in all people.

Spirit is *All the Good There Is.*
Spirit is love, unity, and peace.
Spirit is Karma in action throughout eternity.
Spirit is Infinite Forgiveness.
Spirit is ever-present Evolution.

I AM a unique part of Spirit.
I AM *All the Good There Is.*
I AM love, unity, and peace.
I AM constantly evolving as Karma helps me to increase my awareness of Reality.
My love has no boundaries and forgiveness is a part of me as I AM a part of the Beloved.
I let go of all my human limitations as Allah supports my spiritual evolution.

I AM thankful for the Infinite Law of Mind (Universal Consciousness) that supports my thoughts of love, peace, harmony, and compassion for all people.

As Nature continues to reveal *It's* beauty to me, I release this treatment to the Universal Mind, secure in the Truth of One

Mind, constantly evolving and manifesting *All the Good There Is*.

And So *It* Is!

Weather Conditions Treatment

I AM a manifestation of Pure Spirit, in unity with all things, including the ever-changing weather.

As I recognize my unity with Divine BEing in sunshine, shade, rain, and clouds, strong wind and calm breezes, I enjoy and agree with all weather conditions. Each change in the weather is as welcome to me as the variations in my life. I AM always filled with Divine Love and Harmony. I feel harmonious, spiritually and physically complete. I AM free of fear or confusion for I AM the wind, the clouds, the rain, and the sunshine in the sky. I AM in unity with all weather, one with the heat, the cold, humidity, and dryness of the atmosphere, always changing as my spirit grows.

I AM one with all things. As Nature continues to reveal *It's* beauty to me, I rejoice in freedom, fearlessly weathering all climate changes. While I glaze upon the peaceful calm sky or the beauty of the perfect storm, Divine Mind fills me with joyous gratefulness.

I release these words effortlessly into the atmosphere to flow throughout the vastness of the Universe.

And So *It* Is!

Wholeness and Health

God is present in all things. This Creative Energy flows easily within and through me.

As this Perfect Presence circulates in every cell of my body, it spreads a Divine sense of peace and ease. Spiritual perfection continues to remove all obstructions, barriers in my mind, veins, and life experiences. The flow of Life Force is unretarded filling me with *All the Good There Is*.

I AM grateful for the freely flowing stream of fearless peace that operates through the power of Absolute Law. And I give thanks for the constantly renewed flow of the One Infinite Life and Substance within me.

I release this treatment to the Creative Mind, the Law of God, knowing that Divine Peace and unhindered Life Force is within me forevermore.

And So *It* Is!

Epilogue

I am eternally grateful for the unseen force that guides me effortlessly toward the Light of Reality. All is in Divine Order as I complete the next book from my Heaven on earth.

Using the Law of Mind to create a perfect living environment is enormously rewarding. It's all about monitoring thought patterns. As Ernest Holmes wrote in 1926, disease and poverty cease to exist as we investigate the Truth and put *It* into operation. Enlightenment leads the way to freedom and Heaven on earth. I AM the living proof.

:-)

Resources

Holmes, Ernest. *The Science of Mind*. New York: Penguin Putnam Inc., 1938, 1998. (ernestholmes.wwwhubs.com).

International Centers for Spiritual Living (csl.org).

Because of the dynamic nature of the Internet, any Web addresses or links contained in this book may have changed since publication and may no longer be valid.

About the Author

SAM is a wayshower helping others to learn the truth of their BEing so humanity can return to Source. She is a lifelong believer in the power of Love. Her inspiring life demonstrates the strength of Mind over matter. It's a story of progression from desperation to hope, poverty to riches, limitation to freedom, and fear to Love.

The awareness that we're spirits, in human form having a physical experience, came shortly after April 4, 2004. A quest for self-mastery began in 2005 when the essence of her son led her to the Science of Mind. SAM turned her back on traditional medicine after decades of illness and multiple surgeries. Using Eastern medicine, and the teachings of Ernest Holmes, she successfully rid herself of many maladies.

SAM's book series is a personal account highlighting the process of one Lightworker's awakening. Books from this author include:

Book One: Death of the Sun

Book Two: A Change in Perception

Lightworker's Log :-) Transformation

Manifesting: Lightworker's Log

Prayer Treatments: Lightworker's Log

Adventures in Greece and Turkey

Earth Angels

Return to Light :-) John of God Helps

Bits of Wisdom

Book of One :-) Volume 1

Book of One :-) Volume 2

SAM is administrator of the popular Internet resource, Lightworker's Log (LightworkersLog.com). She currently concentrates on writing and spreading Spirit's message of Oneness throughout the globe. Guided by messages and synchronicities, SAM knows her most valuable asset is the ever-increasing awareness of our true BEing, unique figments of *All That Is*.

www.ingramcontent.com/pod-product-compliance
Lightning Source LLC
Chambersburg PA
CBHW031359040426
42444CB00005B/352